Praise for Martin Lewis

'Martin Lewis, the man behind moneysavingexpert.com, is one of those people who can lead you through big decisions involving huge amounts of money as if they are laughably unscary. He is a modern-day Robin Hood, and I may love him more than Phil Spencer from *Location Location Location*' Katy Guest, *Independent*

'If anyone can help, it's this man. Martin Lewis knows more about credit cards than possibly anyone else in the country' Justin Rowlatt, BBC1 *Panorama*

'Like Nicky Campbell with much bigger balls' *Independent*

'a thorn in the corporate establishment's side' *Sunday Times*

'a highly politicised, single-issue campaigner, working to correct the imbalance of power between companies and their customers' *Daily Telegraph*

'The UK's biggest financial anorak' Paul Lewis, BBC Radio 4's *Moneybox*

Praise for Martin's bestselling *The Money Diet*

'The greatest money-saving book ever written' *The Motley Fool*

'a feast of valuable help' *i*

MARTIN LEWIS

MoneySavingExpert.com

THE THREE MOST IMPORTANT LESSONS YOU'VE NEVER BEEN TAUGHT

Vermilion

LONDON

1 3 5 7 9 10 8 6 4 2

Published in 2008 by Vermilion, an imprint of Ebury Publishing

A Random House Group Company

The Random House Group Limited Reg. No. 954009

Addresses for companies within the Random House Group can be found at
www.randomhouse.co.uk

A CIP catalogue record for this book is available from the British Library

Penguin Random House is committed to a sustainable future for
our business, our readers and our planet. This book is made from
Forest Stewardship Council® certified paper.

Printed and bound in Great Britain by Clays Ltd, Elcograf S.p.A.

ISBN 9780091923846
Copies are available at special rates for bulk orders. Contact the sales
development team on 020 7840 8487 for more information.

To buy books by your favourite authors and register for offers,
visit www.rbooks.co.uk

CONTENTS

P.S. This book will work whether you use the internet or not. Yet throughout there are lots of web-links for further information to help you save money. The internet is a very powerful tool for MoneySaving. So why not go along to your local library, where you can use the web for free and even get lessons in how to do it?

THINGS HAVE
CHANGED SINCE I
WAS AT SCHOOL...

Things have changed since I was at school... but not enough. Companies spend billions of pounds a year on marketing, advertising and training their staff to sell; yet we still don't get any buyers' training.

This means we as consumers are naked in the face of their commerciality. It's time to change that and I've a bunch of 15-year-olds to thank for making me realise that.

Where It All Started

The ITV1 *Tonight* programme gave me a challenge: take a class of ordinary teenagers for one day and turn them into junior MoneySavingExperts. It was a scary concept, and like nothing I'd tried before. Yet the results were astonishing: after class, the 12 pupils went home and saved their families a whopping £5,050!

Think about that. These children, with just a day's worth of lessons, were able to go home and in a significant way rework some elements of their parents' finances. Why? Simple: because as a nation we're close to being illiterate when it comes to finances and debt, and people are scared of money decisions and change. We're taught to be loyal and to listen to the bank manager; we don't prioritise our own finances; and we don't take time to sort them out.

At that point I decided it was time to try and help people change this mindset. Not just for themselves, but for the next generation too. This book is an attempt to break the cycle.

The short lessons contained in these pages are based on what I taught the Teen Cash

Class, and include some of their reactions. Yet don't think that means it's child's play. This isn't a trite guide to 'opening a bank account' or 'how cheques work'. This is a real practical survival guide to living in one of the most competitive consumer economies in the world. In just an hour or so, these three lessons are designed to give you the ability to carefully critique every money action you make.

Fifteen-year-olds learn new concepts every day; they're like sponges waiting to suck up information. Without doubt, that class was far more adaptable than most adults on whom I've done money makeovers in the course of my television career.

So whether this is for you, or even your teen, the real question is... Can you match up to a 15-year-old?

LESSON ONE:

KNOW YOUR ENEMY — A COMPANY ISN'T YOUR FRIEND

Let me say this loud and clear at the start: **know your enemy – a company is not your friend.**

It is the single most important thing I'll say in this whole guide. If you don't understand it, you've lost before you've even started.

Now don't think this means I'm anti-company; I'm not. I don't think they do anything wrong. This is simply a function of how our society works. My problem isn't that their job is to make money; my problem is that most people don't understand this and think instead that businesses are there to help and assist with daily life.

Of course, some companies give a great service, but that's just part of making money.

As a business you can attract customers in many ways: using cheap prices; offering the best product; giving great customer service. Yet these are simply all a way to bring in customers and increase your profits.

Sometimes, the very fact they want your cash works in your favour. If you're a new customer and they want business, you're likely to get a great deal. Yet once you've been trapped into buying a product, you may well find that it's not right for you, but now they've got your money, they don't give a stuff.

Why this lesson is important:

£ Until you understand that a company's job is to make money, you will make the wrong decisions

£ YOU are the only person who is really bothered about YOU

The aim of this lesson isn't to make you 'avoid' companies but to make you 'understand' them, and remember that when they try and sell you something – whether it's a mobile phone or debt – that doesn't mean it's good or bad for you. It means it'll make THEM money.

If you don't learn this lesson, companies will be left with smiles on their faces while you will be left eating cold baked beans at mealtimes because it could be all you can afford. A company's job is to make money; it is NOT there to help you; it is NOT your friend. They spend billions on advertising, marketing and teaching their staff to sell; all to make you part with your cash, even when you shouldn't!

Still unsure about this? Right. Think about a supermarket:

BREAKING THE IMPULSE CHAIN

Okay. Hands up all those who are guilty of impulse shopping: buying something on a whim, without even thinking about it? Shops want you to see something, lose your mind over it and buy it there and then. Surely, by now, you're smarter than that? If you want something you hadn't planned to buy never buy it on the day you spot it, or even the next. Go back and repeat the relevant money mantras all over again. If it's right to buy the thing you want, then go ahead – guilt free. But chances are, with a pause before buying, the impulse to buy will have lessened.

I asked the Teen Cash Class: 'If I were able to give you back all the money you've ever spent buying things on impulse, would you take the cash and hand over the stuff?'

The store layout. Items that you regularly buy – your bread and milk – tend to be sprinkled around the store; so you have to pass by many other tempting goodies to complete your shopping.

Feeling hungry? Delicious food smells regularly waft through the store. Of course, when you're hungry, you buy more food!

Don't look at eye-level. The most profitable stock is placed at eye-level (or children's eye-level if it's targeted at them); yet profitable goods for stores tend not to be the best deals for shoppers, so the adage 'look high and low for something' really does apply here.

Not all sales are 'super!' While grapes and other attractive products may be placed near the front of a store to entice you in with a genuine bargain, the same signage and displays will be used elsewhere to promote deals, yet these mightn't be competitive. Bright colours and the words 'discount' or 'sale' make us feel good, yet the reduction may be pennies, and cheaper equivalent products may still be hidden on the shelf.

£ **Spot the sweets and magazines by the till.** These are impulse buys, so putting them near the till gives the store one last attempt to grab our cash: kids can nag their parents for goodies too.

Everything about this store – everything you can smell, see and hear – is geared towards making you spend; over the years they've honed it to get your money. And this fictional store is virtually identical to every supermarket in Britain; they are cathedrals of consumerism.

This is what you're up against, everywhere you spend! Be aware of it and you automatically start to lessen the impact. Ask yourself, 'Do I really want to buy it, or am I just a victim of their marketing schemes and spending money I'd be better keeping?'

So let's get going – there's no time to lose…

ARE YOU 'GOOD WITH MONEY'?

When I asked the Teen Cash Class this question, quite a few said yes. Their reason was invariably something like, 'I try and save, not spend, when I get cash.' Yet for me, this doesn't make you good with money; it just means you stay within a budget. Being good with cash is just as much about how you spend as whether or not you spend. It's about how well you understand the value of money, and what it can be used for. Can you effectively see through the thousands of companies telling you different things about where to stash it; where to spend it; and what to splurge it on? Which of these two would you say is best with cash?

£ **Sally the Saver.** She has £400 for a holiday. She spends £250 on a budget flight to Rome, and stays in a youth hostel, managing to save £60 of her holiday money.

£ **Silvia the SavvySpender.** She also has £400 for a holiday. She manages to find a bargain business class flight to New York, stays in a nice hotel with a pool and gets discount theatre tickets but spends the whole £400.

The answer depends on your circumstances and what you can use the money for. If

Silvia's in debt, and splashing out on a holiday, she's not good with money even though she got the better bargain. Being cash savvy is about understanding what money you have, and how to use it.

During Lesson One, I hope you'll develop this kind of vision... And learn a few home truths about the society we now live in.

LOOK OUT FOR NUMBER ONE

I really don't want to get all touchy-feely about this, but the first thing for me to really knock into you – really, BANG BANG, knock into you – is that the only person who's ever going to properly help you is YOU.

Here's a very tough truth:

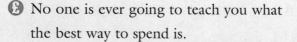 No one is ever going to teach you what the best way to spend is.

£ No one is ever going to write a budget for you, or watch to ensure you stick to it.

£ No one is ever going to tell you the best way to borrow money, should you need to do so.

£ YOU have to learn how to do all these things for yourself.

£ YOU have to become as clever as the companies who are trying to get your cash.

You may think your family or boyfriend/ girlfriend/husband/wife or pet dog may take over your finances for you. But do that and you're following someone else's agenda. That's not good. Cooperating and working together is fine. But you must make your own decisions.

MARTIN'S MONEY MANTRAS

A mantra is something that you repeat to yourself over and over again to help control the way you think. You're about to learn two simple money mantras I developed when I first became the Money Saving Expert. Their job is to slow down the process that makes you spend, so that you're correctly questioning what you're doing.

The Mantra if You're Skint

The first mantra is the one to use when you're skint. Picture yourself with some friends, wandering around your local shopping centre. You're eyeing something up – something that's making your blood rush – and your head thinks, 'I want it! I need it! I must have it!'

Just stop!

Repeat the following mantra to yourself before you get any closer to the sign that reads 'Please Pay Here'. Then repeat it again. And again:

£ **Do I need it?**

£ **Can I afford it?**

£ **Can I get it cheaper somewhere else?**

£ **If you don't need it, don't buy it.**
   If you buy something you don't need, it's obviously a waste of money.

£ **If you can't afford it, don't buy it.**
   If you buy something you can't afford, you begin a cycle of living beyond your means. Eventually, you'll have to borrow money to do this, and you could end up in debt crisis.

£ **If you can afford it, check and make sure that the same thing isn't available**

at a better price somewhere else. Look in other shops, and use the internet to search for the best deal (more on this in Lesson Three). If you haven't checked, don't buy it (yet).

The Mantra if You're Not Skint

The second mantra is for those of you who aren't totally broke. I know what you're thinking: 'Why do I need a money mantra if I've got enough cash?' Two reasons:

£ COMPANIES ARE NOT YOUR FRIENDS (as if I need to remind you). They are after your cash and do not care if they give you a good deal.

£ To make sure that YOU are in control of your spending, NOT THEM! If you don't think carefully about every money decision you make, you are

giving those devious advertising gurus
back their power. You are doing their job
for them.

Time to imagine a scenario again. You've
got some money in your wallet, you're
feeling good and you've got your eye on
something special. You know what's
coming...

Just stop! Ask yourself the following three
questions:

🢒 **Will I use it?**
🢒 **Is it worth it?**
🢒 **Can I get it cheaper somewhere else?**

There arc important differences between this
mantra and the one for those who are skint.
Here, the questions focus on whether it's
going to be a good buy, not whether you
should buy.

If you've bought something and you

never use it when you get home, is that a
good deal?

Next, even more importantly, you need to
ask yourself whether it's worth the amount it
costs. Consider this Teen Cash Class example:

Alexandra:
A good friend bought some shoes once
that cost £100.

Martin:
Did she need them?

Alexandra:
Well… She said she needed some new shoes.

Martin:
Could she afford them?

Alexandra:
I think so. She had quite a lot of money,
so she could afford to spend that much.

Martin:

Could she have got them cheaper somewhere else?

Alexandra:

Oh no, definitely not. They were one pair of shoes from a certain place, not available anywhere else.

Martin:

Did she use them?

Alexandra:

Well, I think she's worn them about three times...

Martin:

So, were they worth it?

Difficult, isn't it? Is three times, or £33 per use, good enough to justify buying them in the first place? Could she have got more use or more enjoyment by spending £100 on something else? Ultimately, only Alexandra's friend will know that – but it's crucial to consider this before buying anything.

The fancy term that economists use for this dilemma is '**opportunity cost**'. This is where you have one thing but, as a result, miss out on having another. You don't have to be a genius to assess opportunity cost, though – you can do it yourself, every time you shop, by asking yourself honestly: 'Is it worth it?'

As always, everything comes back to you in the end. YOU have to remember these mantras. YOU have to apply them. If you do and you're honest with yourself, then these mantras should ensure you don't spend what you haven't got, and you always buy well.

No prizes for guessing what their answer was…'YES!'

Some of them realised they'd spent hundreds of pounds on things they just didn't ever really use. Take a look at those numbers over a full adult working life, and suddenly waste isn't counted in the hundreds, but in the tens of thousands of pounds.

Sadly, in real life, no one will ever make you that offer; so you have to do it in advance by not buying on impulse. Often, impulse control is considered a curmudgeonly act; yet actually it's the opposite. So open up your cupboards, flog the stuff you don't ever use – whether on eBay or at car-boot sales – and use a bit of impulse control to ensure that, from now on, if you won't use it, you won't buy it.

Take Fashion: Do You Really Think It's about Clothes?

Business pervades every element of our lives, yet we've become inured to its charms. We take for granted certain parameters, such as fashion. Does it change every season by accident?

This may shock you, but fashion – rather than being the epitome of cool – is actually one of the most profitable business mechanisms ever invented. Think about it. If we didn't have changing fashions, you'd be able to have a wardrobe full of clothes that you could wear for your whole adult life; and would only ever need changing if they wore out or you changed shape.

Sadly, the billions poured into fashion trendsetting mean it's impossible to ignore. Magazines, television programmes, newspapers, adverts, radio and the web all like to pump out the 'latest trends'. Think about this from the point of view of clothes manufacturers and retailers: 'The stuff they bought six weeks ago can't be worn any more. Yippee! They'll have to spend more with us!'

In a nutshell, fashion changes to make you buy more stuff!

So be careful when buying things that are the 'height of fashion', as it means you won't be able to wear or use them for long. Ask yourself, 'Is it worth it?' Even legendary French fashion designer, Yves Saint-Laurent, admitted, 'Fashion fades; style is eternal.' So buying things to last is better value; and if it's high fashion, make sure it's super-cheap because the value per wear will be tiny. Don't forget...
A COMPANY'S JOB IS TO MAKE MONEY. I cannot say this often enough.

Take this exchange:

Martin:
So come on, are any of you impulse purchasers? Tell the truth...

Sarah:

Well, yeah. I've impulse-bought quite a lot of things.

Martin:

Such as?

Sarah:

Clothes, mostly. Things that I'd just wear once. Really, I could have done something better with that money.

Martin:

How many times do you think you've done that?

Sarah:

Oh, wow, too many times!

Martin:

Twenty? Thirty?

Sarah:

Um, yeah, probably.

Martin:

And how much do you spend each time?

Sarah:

Um, not really a lot. About £20.

Martin:

Robert, you said you were good at maths.
Twenty quid times 30 impulse purchases
makes?

Robert:

Six hundred quid.

Martin:

Right. Sarah, how much pocket money do
you get?

Sarah:

Fifty quid pocket money and £50 for
work every month.

Martin:

So you've spent six months' worth of your
cash – including money you've worked for
– on stuff you didn't really need or want.

Sarah:

Wow! Um, what were those money
mantras again?

If you didn't think that handling your money
well was about a battle between you and the
companies, I hope you've cottoned on by
now. Don't just take my word for it, though.
If you've ever watched the television
programme *Dragons' Den*, take that as further
proof. When assessing the contestants'
business pitches, the panel never ask, 'How
much good will it do society?' Their key

question is, 'Will it make me money?' That's the first priority of any business. There's a reason the programme isn't called *Fluffy Bunnies' Den*!

And you have to remember this: it means that in your dealings with a company you must consider them to be the opposition. While they may be subtly smiling, their job is to outfox you and get as much of your cash as possible. Your job is to stop them.

MoneySaving Web Resources

Here are a few places to find extra hints and tips that will help you use the things you've learnt from Lesson One. If you want to save yourself money, these are the best places to start:

💷 The Demotivator. A special tool to help you stop spending:
www.moneysavingexpert.com/stopspending

💷 A complete money makeover:
www.moneysavingexpert.com/money makeover

💷 Cutting the cost of food shopping:
www.moneysavingexpert.com/supermarket shopping

💷 Are you spending more than you earn?
www.moneysavingexpert.com/budgeting

LESSON TWO:

DEBT – THE TERRIFYING TRUTH

When people need to borrow money, some go to their bank and expect that someone there will tell them the best thing for them to do. Wipe this ridiculous idea from your mind right away. A bank isn't there to give advice; it's there to sell you things and make fat profits.

Whether or not to go into debt, and who to borrow money from, are two of the most important decisions you'll make in your adult life. Yet there is no one who will sit down with you and independently advise or help you with these questions. People will be trying to flog you debt. You could get yourself into trouble this way – and you could be paying for it for 40 years! (No joke – read on.)

Why this lesson is important:

€ There's very little chance you'll be able to live your life without borrowing money at some point - whether it's for university, a house or something else that you need.

€ Logic has changed over the years. While previous generations may have said 'don't ever borrow', this is no longer feasible. We now live in a different world and so need to be equipped with the tools that work.

€ Get debt wrong and it'll cost you a fortune. Unlike most other things we spend cash on, you can't cancel your debts, so you need to get it right first time.

€ More people lead miserable lives because of debt than any other single factor.

WHAT IS DEBT?

Put simply, debt is where you borrow money from someone else, so you now owe them money and have to pay it back. You may have already been in debt at some point – to your parents, partner, friends or family. But when you borrow from a company, it's not like borrowing a fiver from your sister and giving it back to her next week when you can afford to. A company, such as a bank or credit card firm, will want your fiver back PLUS more on top.

It's their payment for lending you the money AND they'll want the debt repaid in a certain way at a certain time, to suit them. Miss this at your peril because your costs and troubles will mount up. Let's not forget: **banks are not your friends.**

AN INTERESTING PROBLEM

The most important thing to understand about debt is how interest works and just how clever it is. The 'interest' is the cost of borrowing money and is often displayed in a way that makes it look cheap but in fact makes lenders a fortune. As you're about to discover, it's pure genius; the same number can be both cheap and expensive. If you don't learn to understand it, prepare to stand in the road and empty out your pockets as you'll end up giving them your money anyway.

The Interest Rate

This is the cost you pay for having debt, expressed as a percentage of the amount you borrowed that you will have to pay back on top of the original borrowing. Normally this is the cost per year but it isn't always – so always check.

Typically, if you borrow money on a credit card, it will charge you around 18 per cent interest a year. The actual way it works is quite complex, so I'm going to simplify it for the moment...

Are Percentages a Struggle for You?
Of course, my Teen Cash Class were 15-year-olds on the verge of GCSE maths; so for them, percentages were as easy as operating the remote control. Sadly, in adult life many lose such basic maths skills, so let me briefly recap for those who may have forgotten:

Borrow £1,000 at 18 per cent over a year
The amount you must repay equals the original
= £1,000

Plus the interest (18 per cent of £1,000) = £180
Total: £1,180

One percentage point of something is the same as saying one hundredth of it.

Using the above example, we could also say 18 per cent is eighteen hundredths of the amount (written in decimals as 0.18 of the amount). Therefore, to find out what this equals, first find out what one hundredth is.

To do this, you divide the amount (£1,000) by 100. Here the answer is £10.

Now you multiply it by the number of percentage points.

We need to know what 18 per cent of it is, so we simply multiply one hundredth (£10) by 18 to find out. The answer is £180.

From here on in, I'm going to assume you understand percentages.

The Amount You Pay Isn't Just about the Interest Rate

This is one of the big ones; one that many people get wrong. They only consider the interest rate when deciding how to borrow, yet there's another big factor: how long you borrow for.

Look at this example from my Teen Cash Class: Callum was quick – he understood that you don't just pay interest; you also have to pay interest on the interest. This is called 'compound interest' and it makes lenders a fortune. Albert Einstein, no less, described compound interest as one of the world's most powerful forces.

Let's briefly look at why… borrowing £1,000 at 20 per cent:

£ *After year 1:*
You owe £1,000 for the original debt, plus £200 interest.

£ *After year 2:*

You owe £1,200 from last year plus £200 interest on the original borrowing and £40 interest on the interest = £1,440.

£ *After year 3*:

You owe £1,440 from last year plus £200 interest on the original borrowing, and £80 interest on the interest and £8 interest on the interest on the interest = £1,728.

As you can see, each year the cost of your borrowing increases, and it accelerates so that it costs much more the longer you borrow. So much so that...

Martin:

I borrow £1,000 from the bank at an interest rate of 20 per cent over one year. How much does it cost me?

Callum:
£200.

Martin:
Get your calculators out now. What about this: the same debt, at the same rate, over two years.

Callum:
£440.

Martin:
Right. The amount you have to pay back has increased.

£ *After year 20:*
If compound interest didn't exist, so you only paid interest on the original borrowing, you'd have to repay £5,000; but because of compound interest, you actually need to repay a huge... **£38,400!** All this means that the longer you borrow for, the more it costs you.

I'm sure you've seen the television ads that say things like, 'Shift all of your debts to us and we'll give you a low rate.' Well, guess what? These companies are not your friends! They will end up making more profit from you, because to get the low rate you must repay over a much, much longer time, so they earn masses in interest.

Always remember, a lower interest rate doesn't guarantee cheaper borrowing. If you're going to borrow money, you have to ask the question, 'How long am I going to borrow for?' as well as, 'What's the rate of interest?'

MoneySaving Web Resource

For more on the different types of interest rates visit:

www.moneysavingexpert.com/interestrates

Mistaken Identity: 'Is a Lower Rate for Longer Cheaper than a Short-term High Rate?'

Imagine you have a mortgage and, because the lender is secure in the knowledge it can take the house back if you can't repay, it gives you a cheap rate at, say, 6 per cent.

Now you need an additional loan for a car and the best interest rate you can find is 12 per cent. Suddenly, your mortgage lender says, 'Hey! Why not borrow that extra £10,000 on top of your mortgage? After all, at 6 per cent, it's half price.'

This is a classic scenario and, sadly erroneous, logic always pushes for 'low rate is cheap'. Thus, instinctively and unthinking, we tend to head towards that. The Teen Cash Class selected this option. Faced with the same dilemma, most adults do the same.

Yet crunch the numbers and it works out that a typical loan will be paid back over five years, whereas most mortgages last for 25 years. And you have to take this into account.

Here's the real answer:

£ A £10,000 loan at 12 per cent over five years costs £3,300 in interest.

£ £10,000 added to a mortgage at 6 per cent over 25 years costs £9,200 in interest.

As you can see, the higher interest rate loan is much cheaper, though it means you have to repay more a month because it needs to be repaid more quickly.

GOOD DEBT, BAD DEBT... AND KNOWING THE DIFFERENCE

You now understand what debt is. It's important to realise that, as nasty as it can be (and trust me, sometimes it is), you are not going to be able to avoid it. So what's important is learning when it's right to borrow, and to understand the best way to do it.

Let me start with a quick quiz I gave the Teen Cash Class. Which of these do you think are examples of good and bad debt?

A. You want to go on holiday because you haven't been away for three months, but you'd need to pay for it on a credit card.

Good debt or bad debt?

B. You recently got married and now it's time to buy your own house. You need to borrow money by getting a mortgage in order to do so.

Good debt or bad debt?

C. You've just got a new job and moved house. You live eight miles from work and your children go to a school ten miles away. There's no public transport, so you borrow money for a car.

Good debt or bad debt?

D. You have a store card with a limit of £500, and you're off to a big party tonight. You see some top party clothes that cost £250, so you go for it.

Good debt or bad debt?

Of course, no debt is truly 'good', as you don't want to borrow anything from anyone, but 'necessary and unnecessary debt' was too long a phrase! See page 109 for the answers.

Now let me show you one of the most important real-life examples of good debt and bad debt:

The 'Good Debt, Bad Debt' of Student Borrowing

The introduction of student loans in the UK was a national tragedy. Don't think I'm making a political point here – my issue isn't with the fact that loans exist. My problem is that modern Britain is now a place where we educate our young people *into* debt, but never *about* debt. When introducing a nationwide enforced borrowing programme, how did we miss the opportunity to start explaining to people how debt works?

And it's for this reason I think it's beholden on all of us – whether students, parents, grandparents or opt-outs living in an isolated commune – to understand student debt. As a side benefit, it offers some great insights into how to spot good debt and bad debt generally.

There are three types of student borrowing on offer. Crazy as it sounds, they're radically different and no one bothers to explain this before students head off to university:

💷 **Official student loans**. The government gives you this loan to cover your tuition fees and some living costs. It's set at the rate of inflation (the rate at which prices rise), making it the cheapest form of long-term debt possible. Even better, you don't need to start repaying it until you're earning over £15,000, and then the less you earn the less you repay.

€ **Interest-free overdrafts.** Most banks offer these to higher education students. An overdraft is an amount of money pre-agreed between you and your bank that you can withdraw from your account when there is no cash in it. Many banks like to allow students to borrow for free, because this attracts them as customers.* This means that, while you study, the money you borrow doesn't cost you any cash – but they will want you to pay it back in instalments from when your course finishes, and may begin to charge you interest.

* *Don't think banks are being generous by doing this! The idea is that they get you as a student and then once you finish, you end up not moving to another bank for life – even though you'll get better rates elsewhere. In fact, it's a very cheap way of them buying your custom! Always remember: once you finish university or college, look again for the best new bank.*

£ **Commercial debts**. This is all other types of debt including credit cards, store cards, additional loans and hire purchase agreements. On this kind of debt, you will be paying real, expensive interest that will build up and not go away.

Now, of the three types of debt on offer, it's obvious that the official Student Loan is the best. This is a great example of good debt. A university degree is something that can be considered an investment in your future – it's not the same as slapping a new pair of shoes on a store card. More importantly, by borrowing from the government you're getting the best available deal in terms of interest and repayments.

More confusingly is how we evaluate the interest-free overdraft. In the short term, this might seem like good debt – perhaps you need the money to survive and, after all, you're not paying interest. However, it can very easily become bad debt if it isn't paid off correctly; your bank can begin charging you interest, and before you know it what once was free ends up costing you a bundle.

Getting into commercial debt while you're at university is definitely the worst pick from the choices above. In fact, I'd go as far as to say never, ever, ever, ever take this type of borrowing.

How Does a Student Not Spend More than They Earn?

The three types of debt listed here provoke an even more interesting money dilemma. With adults, the rule is simple: over the long run, 'don't spend more than you earn'. Yet what shouldn't students 'spend more than'? They don't earn anything and borrowing is enforced. I remember asking this question during a speech to a conference of debt-advisers and even they were stumped. We never think beyond the conventional rules.

The answer, in my view, is: 'add up your student loan, any income from working and any money from parents and don't spend more than that; perhaps using your 0 per cent overdraft but only for cash flow'. In our society, young people *need* to budget based on borrowing, which is why we've no option but to say debt isn't bad, but bad debt is bad.

The Debt Spiral... When Borrowing Gets Ugly

One of the most dangerous things you can do with money is consistently spend more than you earn, and borrow to fill the gap. Unfortunately, many people just spend willy-nilly on credit cards, without ever thinking where the money to repay them will come from. The risk here is that you enter a debt spiral – and this is where bad debt turns really ugly. It stands to reason that, the more money you borrow, the higher your

repayments will be every month. This means
that, to carry on living in the same way, you
borrow a bit more. Then a bit more…

Some people may tell you to avoid all
borrowing. My view – and not everyone agrees
– is that we have to grow up and understand
that borrowing is an unwelcome, but
necessary, part of life. That's why my aim isn't
to scare you off ever borrowing, but to show
you how scary – if done badly – it can be. Yet
if you plan it; check it's worthwhile; budget for
it; understand it; and ensure it's as cheap and
affordable as possible then it isn't always bad.

The old-fashioned attitude of 'never
borrow' can actually be dangerous.
Grandparents trying to force this onto their
student grandchildren, rather than educating
them about how to borrow, can do more harm
than help. If you think that all borrowing is
bad, but you're forced to borrow, there's no
difference between good and bad debt, so it's
easier to get the bad type. Let's lose the stigma

Don't Get Into a Debt Spiral

You spend more than you earn

 You borrow to fill the gap

More of your income goes
towards repaying debts

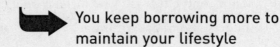 You keep borrowing more to
maintain your lifestyle

THE END RESULT

 All your income goes
towards repaying debt

YOU'VE NOTHING LEFT

of borrowing, but understand that there is such a thing as bad borrowing. When you've nothing left, you're in debt crisis and this is when things get catastrophic.

People get divorced; people have their homes taken away because they can no longer afford their mortgage; some people even threaten to kill themselves. ALL of these things can be the results of a debt spiral – a spiral that might start off very small.

Now this probably sounds scary to you. And it should. I want it to scare you. I helped my Teen Cash Class to understand it this way:

Martin:

If you enjoy going to the cinema every week but suddenly can't afford it, what do you do?

Teen Cash Class:

Well, you stop going to the cinema. If you've arranged it, you cancel it.

Martin:

Right, but what about debts? What if you suddenly don't have enough money to repay your debts? You can't stop that. You can't cancel that. You can't run away from it. That's the difference between debts and other spending – once you've got them, you can't stop them!

If you currently have debt problems, then you need to act urgently. Debt doesn't go away if you forget about it. See the full debt problems checklist at:
www.moneysavingexpert.com/debtproblems

If your debts are so severe that you can't meet even the minimum repayments, you've moved into 'debt crisis'. In this case, and only in this case, you need to adopt a totally different strategy. This means looking to negotiate with your creditors and go for debt management. Yet don't do it with commercial companies as, unsurprisingly, their prime job is to make money from you. Instead, go to one of the free, non-profit agencies listed below.

Debt Counselling Web Resources

💷 Consumer Credit Counselling Service:
www.cccs.co.uk Tel: 0800 138 1111

💷 National Debtline:
www.nationaldebtline.co.uk
Tel: 0808 808 4000

💷 Citizens Advice Bureau:
www.adviceguide.org.uk

CREDIT CARDS

I've already mentioned these in passing. Now it's time for me to devote my full attention to them.

There's no more important single product to learn about than credit cards. In my view we'd all be better off if these were renamed 'debt cards' rather than credit cards as they're designed to make us borrow money.

Sadly, many people have a big misunderstanding about credit cards and their cousins, store cards. So it's time for those big, bold letters again:

£ **Credit cards do NOT give you free money!**

£ **You have to pay back every penny you spend...**
  AND A WHOLE LOT MORE.

£ **Interest charges on credit cards can be EXTREME!**

A credit card is just a pre-approved loan, so once you've got it you can borrow as much as you like from it, up to a set limit. Yet just like a loan, every penny needs to be paid back... and if they don't get their cash and their interest, they'll come for you. The key difference between borrowing in the form of a loan and using a credit card is that with a credit card you decide how much (or how little) you pay off per month. In addition, you decide how much you borrow, within a pre-arranged limit.

Already, you should be able to hear alarm bells!

£ You can continually borrow more each month than you have to repay. There's no pressure on you to pay a lot of money back, so you could easily end up borrowing more and more cash until it's unaffordable.

£ It's incredibly difficult to budget with a credit card, and your spending can quickly get out of control.

If you want to admire innovative money-making genius, take a look at credit card minimum repayments. Like sharks, they're deadly but beautiful. The credit card minimum repayment system is one of the most ingenious money-making schemes ever devised. You have to admire the companies for thinking this one up because it truly is outstandingly profitable, and, better still for them, most people don't notice it!

Remember, with credit cards you are in control of the repayments, and all you have to do each month is meet the minimum amount they've set. This is usually around 2 per cent of the total debt or £5 (whichever is the greater).

Now prepare to be truly terrified by this example of how minimum repayments work, which the Teen Cash Class worked through:

Imagine that you owe £3,000 on a credit card. It's at an interest rate of 17.9 per cent, which is quite typical. The minimum repayment on that card, at 2 per cent, would be £60.

Martin:
Right. Imagine that you're going to pay just the minimum payment every month – starting at £60 – until the debt's paid off. How long is it going to take until the debt's paid off?

Jack:
A year?

Martin:
Hmm, a year. Who thinks between one and three years? Some of you.

Who thinks three to five years? Five to seven? Some more of you.

Seven to ten years? Ten to fifteen years? Has anyone not put their hand up?

What if I told you that it would take you 40 years to pay off that debt? At a cost of £6,300 in interest? Does that shock you?

Yup, you read it right the first time: IT'D
TAKE 40 YEARS TO REPAY! You'd all be
grey before it was repaid!

Teen Cash Class:
Wow! I don't believe it! (Mouths were
hanging open, including that of the teacher
who was supervising at the back of the class,
the two cameramen, the sound operators,
the producer and the assistant producer!)

MoneySaving Web Resource

To work out exactly how long your
credit cards will take to repay, use the minimum
repayment calculator at:
www.moneysavingexpert.com/minrepayments

Imagine you start getting into this debt at the
age of around 20, and you settle for making
the minimum payment each month. You're

going to be **60** by the time that debt is cleared!

Why does this happen? Here's the secret of minimum repayments:

The minimum repayment is set as a **percentage** of what you owe. Therefore, as the amount you owe decreases so does the amount you need to pay back.

Worse still, the minimum repayment is set as an amount that only just covers the interest you owe (which is also set as a percentage), and thus you're hardly paying back any of the original amount you borrowed. Clever, innit?

Credit card companies designed minimum repayments to trap you into debt for the rest of your life. They want to see you take 40 years to pay it off as that way they earn a mass of interest and you're permanently in debt to them.

Don't worry, though. I've a stick to hit them back with, as the Teen Cash Class found out:

Martin:

Okay. So imagine now that instead of letting the amount you pay each month reduce, you fix the amount you pay at £60 each month, the same as the minimum payment in the first month. How long is it going to take you now to clear the debt?

Callum:

A few years?

Martin:

Seven years. You will pay £2,300 in interest, saving yourself £4,000 – and you clear the debt 33 years earlier.

Think about why this is so effective...
The amount you repay is fixed. Thus, while the debt and interest decrease, your repayments stay firm. The interest drops, but more of your money goes towards

repaying the actual debt rather than the interest.

Credit Cards Aren't All Bad

At this point, you probably feel that credit cards are fairly terrible things. I should perhaps say in their defence that, used correctly, they can actually be good. Using a credit card, for example, is often the cheapest way to spend abroad, and with some cards you can earn cashback every time you buy something. Plus, if you need to borrow, the right credit cards are the very cheapest way.

Yet like so many things, though, a credit card can turn nasty in the wrong hands. Remember, as always, the responsibility to do the smart thing ultimately lies with **YOU**.

The Teen Cash Class Credit Card Challenge

This was the challenge my Teen Cash Class found the most difficult, but also the most enjoyable.

Here's a real-life scenario... Imagine you have £2,500 on a Barclaycard at 16 per cent interest, and have done for a few years, and you also need to borrow £1,000 for stuff for a new home.

What's the best credit card solution you can come up with?

Now what? The Teen Cash Class had to go to different banks and find leaflets to compare offers, yet you can do the same on the internet.

Call me a soppy old git (go on if you like, I can't hear you), but doing this with the Teen Cash Class nearly brought me to tears. It's because, at one moment, I suddenly looked at them and saw them all quietly studying credit card leaflets. Having spent most of my career trying to explain to people how they're being ripped off, the one thing I know most people haven't done is actually sit down and examine different deals. To see my Teen Cash Class doing it, and enjoying it, was a wonderful moment. Better still was how they started realising there are vast differences between cards.

What's the answer? Credit card deals change all the time, so it depends on when you do this. Yet the process of comparing credit cards to try and find the winning deal is the best lesson possible. Here are some hints:

💷 **All cards aren't the same**. While they're the same shape and size, the rates and deals on credit cards differ massively. So ensure you read the small print and check exactly what the terms are.

£ **They're a tool, not an accessory.** Don't ever be drawn into picking a credit card for its colour or design, and forget gimmicks or cards linked to football teams or funky stores. These are ways to draw you in. Always compare cards based on which is financially best for you.

£ **There's more than one interest rate.** One card may have a number of different interest rates. The two main ones are for 'purchases' – for new spending on the card – and 'balance transfers', which is a special offer if you move debt from a previous credit card to it.

£ **It's not about getting 'one card'.** Don't assume that you're looking for one credit card. It's often better to get two cards: one for the cheapest purchases debt and one for the cheapest balance transfers. There's no 'one-size-fits-all' deal.

MoneySaving Web Resources

I've only just opened the door to credit cards. There's so much more to learn. If you do the above properly you're going to have a lot of questions about the different types of deals out there. And don't worry, the answers exist. For much more on credit cards use the following resources:

(£) Best balance transfers: how to cut the cost of debts on existing cards: www.moneysavingexpert.com/bts

(£) Best card for purchases: if you need to borrow on a credit card, how to pick the best: www.moneysavingexpert.com/purchases

(£) Newbies' guide to credit cards: the different card types: www.moneysavingexpert.com/ccnewbies

THE FINAL INSULT

I've spent this whole lesson talking about
debts. And I want to explain one final thing
to you before I finish, which takes us back to
Lesson One – a company's job is to make
money from us...

When you borrow money from the bank
in whatever form, it charges you interest.
When you save with a bank, you are paid
interest. This is because you are actually
lending the bank your own money – and
so it's also paying you interest.

But now let's look at the different rates.
Imagine you're not a MoneySaver and didn't
bother to check for the best deals (though, of
course, by now I know you would):

£ Put money in a typical bank account and
it pays 0.1 per cent interest.

Put £1,000 in there and you earn £1 a
year (yes, a measly £1).

£ Borrow money on a typical credit card
and it charges 18 per cent interest.
Borrow £1,000 from there and you pay
£180 per year.

It's pretty clever when you think about it:
you lend them money and they give you
diddly-squat back, but if they lend you
money, it costs more. Banks have this rather
unfair interest game entirely in their favour,
and it will stay that way unless you play it
properly.

Worse still, some people will have £1,000
in the bank, and then borrow £1,000 from
the same bank's credit cards! It's madness,
but it's very common. It means the bank gets
to lend you back the money you've lent it –
and make £179 for doing it.

People do this because they like to 'feel I've some money in the bank'. Of course this is a false feeling because if you add up what the person has – and what they owe – they've got nothing. They'd be far better off just spending the money in the bank; that way, at least, they won't be paying any interest on borrowing.

Stooze On!

Now, remember what I just said about banks having the interest game all their own way? For the very sophisticated, there's a game called 'stoozing' where you can get your own back on the banks and play the interest game. And, amazingly, it cropped up during my Teen Cash Class.

The best question any of the teens asked me came after we'd finished filming the credit card challenge. It boiled down to something like this:

Jack:

Martin, if you can borrow money interest-free for a year on a credit card, can't you take this money and put it in a good savings account and earn interest on it?

Martin:

Yes, yes, woo-hoo, wonderful, fab, brilliant. I can't believe you thought of it, I love it!

As you may just be able to tell, I was shocked and delighted they'd figured this out – as most adults never get close to it. If you're super-savvy and in control of your money, it is possible to make money out of credit cards. Some people make big cash (you'll need to be at least 18, though). Stoozing works, yet it's only for those who really know what they're doing.

MoneySaving Web Resource

£ A guide to stoozing:

www.moneysavingexpert.com/stooze

Debt Is Less about Stoozing and More about Thinking...

My reason for including Jack's inspiring comments is less about the practical point of how to stooze and far more about thinking. Debt isn't that complex, but we don't turn our brains to it.

We accept the financial industry's logic. I've lost count of the number of times I've been asked, 'Should I consolidate my debts into one payment?' I'm sure if I said that to 15-year-old Jack, he'd say, 'What's the point of having it all in one place? Surely the aim is to keep your debts as cheap as possible?'

As a nation we've successfully learnt *to* borrow. Now it's time we learnt *how* to borrow.

ONE SIMPLE RULE IF YOU STILL FIND ALL THIS CONFUSING

The thing you must understand after Lesson Two is this: I am not anti-debt. I'm not someone who says that all debt is bad. However, bad debt is very bad!

YOU have to make sure you know the difference between good debt and bad debt. Use my money mantras at all times (*see page 18*), and use the masses of information you've been given during this lesson to make the right decisions about any money you borrow.

Yet there's one final rule: if you *still* don't understand debt, don't get into it. It's as simple as that.

MoneySaving Web Resources

- 💷 How interest rates work:
  www.moneysavingexpert.com/interestrates
- 💷 Should I pay off debts with savings?
  www.moneysavingexpert.com/savingsvsdebts
- 💷 Danger! Minimum repayments (includes minimum repayment calculator):
  www.moneysavingexpert.com/minrepayments
- 💷 Newbies' guide to credit cards:
  www.moneysavingexpert.com/ccnewbies
- 💷 The best balance transfers:
  www.moneysavingexpert.com/bts
- 💷 Store cards: leave them or beat them:
  www.moneysavingexpert.com/storecards
- 💷 The best bank accounts:
  www.moneysavingexpert.com/bankaccounts
- 💷 Debt problems? What to do, where to get help:
  www.moneysavingexpert.com/debtproblems

LESSON THREE:

LOYALTY IS FOR LOSERS — HOW TO BE A SAVVY SHOPPER

The first thing you need to learn in this chapter is that, when it comes to cash, forget all the touchy-feely stuff you've ever been told about how important it is to be loyal. With friends, relatives, husbands, wives? Yes. Loyalty in these relationships is generally a very good plan. But in your dealings with companies, businesses and banks? NO. The average adult in this country wastes up to £5,000 each year – simply by being apathetic and not getting off their backside to grab the best deal.

I'll say it again: LOYALTY IS NEVER REWARDED!

Why this lesson is important:

(£) The normal rules do not apply – sticking with the same people for longer means you get less.

(£) There is no such thing as a 'fixed price'.

(£) No one else will ever search and find the best deal for you.

So ask yourself the question, 'Do I want to be the customer who has companies fighting for my business or do I just want to be taken for granted?'

WHY THE LOYAL LOSE OUT

What you'll actually get, if you're loyal to companies, is usually a bum deal. That's because **companies are not your friends** (have I mentioned that yet?!). By staying with the same company – whether it's a building society, an insurance firm or even your mobile phone provider – you probably think you're doing the right thing. As you'll see below, most members of the Teen Cash Class believed that in return for being a loyal customer, they'd get better treatment.

Martin:

So, imagine you've got a car and you've had insurance with the same firm for years. You've always paid on time, you've never had any problems, but your premium's coming up for renewal. Are you going to get a better deal by sticking with the guys you know or switching to a different company?

Jessica:

I think you probably stay with the one you've been with, so you get more things, like no-claims bonuses.

Robert:

I'd stay with them because if you went to a new company you'd have to start building that up again from scratch... But if you're a loyal customer, you'll get more bonuses.

Martin:

Who agrees? A few of you. Hmm... Think from the insurance company's perspective now. Think – who is the easiest customer to get for their business?

As the conversation progressed, we talked through the simple logic of our dilemma. The answer became obvious:

Jack:

The existing customer. They won't want all the hassle of changing to a different company, and having to make phone calls and send letters out and everything.

Martin:
Right. And if you're an insurance company, how do you win new customers?

Jack:
By bringing them good deals.

Martin:
Good. What else do you have to do to win them over?

Jack:
Advertise, marketing and all that stuff.

Martin:
And that costs money, right? How do you think they cover the cost of giving new customers money off and putting adverts on the telly? Who does that cost get passed on to – I mean, who really ends up footing the bill?

Jack:
The existing customer.

Martin:
Brilliant!

Callum:
The existing customer doesn't cost them anything, either. They don't have to advertise to get them, and they needn't cut their bills.

The amount of feedback I get from people who use my cheaper car insurance system never fails to amaze me. They say something like, 'I can't believe it. I tried your system and it was £200 cheaper, but bizarrely it's with the company I'm currently with.' This shouldn't be a surprise: enter your details as a new customer and it'll fight for your business, but at renewal it's seducing you into apathy.

Changing attitudes about loyalty is a slow process. Getting rid of the concept of the

1950s bank manager in his hat, ready to help you, is crucial. If you haven't got it yet, perhaps it's time to reread the first lesson... a company's job is to make money.

THE APATHY TRAP

So far, so simple. Loyalty doesn't pay, and now you understand why. What's a lot more difficult to explain is the behaviour of millions of people every year who, in the situation outlined above, would simply sign the renewal forms sent by their current insurance provider and wave goodbye to another fat chunk of their hard-earned cash.

These sorry individuals, poor fools, have fallen into what I call the apathy trap. This is where you become thoughtless, you settle into a routine and – in the end – become too lazy to get off your backside and check whether or not you are being swizzed.

It's easily done, you could say: adult life is busy, you have a job, a house to organise, maybe even kids to keep under control. These are all excuses I've heard time and time again. In the end, though, there is no excuse: apathy is the enemy, and as we learnt in Lesson One, you have to do this or no one else will do it for you.

This means, for example, that six weeks before your insurance is up for renewal you put a note in your diary – then you take yourself by the scruff of the neck and make yourself spend some time finding a great price.

SAVVY SHOPPING

The internet has changed the world of shopping and money. That's because there are so many tools out there which offer to do the job for you. Many websites quickly search

the internet to find you the cheapest price.
While of course my 15-years-olds have been
clicking a mouse since before they could read
and found this the easiest exercise of all, for
those with the odd grey hair, it isn't always
as simple. Yet there's no greater single
MoneySaving exercise available than getting
online and web-savvy.

However, while the internet is a great
resource, it's also dangerous. As you've
seen from credit cards, there's no one best
fit deal for anything. So you really must
understand how a product works before
doing a comparison.

Having taught my Teen Cash Class about
car insurance, I then challenged them to find
a better car insurance deal for their history
teacher. Those bright sparks quickly used
their computers to save him a massive £385!
As you already know, they later used their
learning to help their families save thousands
of pounds as well.

Yet they were rightly wary about using the internet. So here are some quick rules:

£ **Always use more than one comparison site**. Even comparison services are commercial companies out to make a profit. They tend to compare only companies who pay them if you end up getting the best deal through them. This means you should use more than one – after all, it doesn't take much time. Take car insurance, for example: even the website which gives the widest search compares only around 30 companies, but if you use four comparison sites you can get around 90 compared and it only takes a few minutes longer.

£ **You may be able to beat the best price by haggling**. Secondly, when you've found a good price, ring the company who are offering it direct and see if you can beat it down some more (details on how to go about this later).

And there are other ways you can use the internet to save yourselves loads of cash. Hundreds of shopping robot websites (shopbots) are now out there, and any one of them could help you save. Whether it's a CD, DVD, book, stereo, skincare product or more, there are comparison engines to search for them for you.

MoneySaving Web Resources

💲 Cheapest car insurance, including a list of comparison sites:
www.moneysavingexpert.com/carins

💲 Cheapest home insurance, including a list of comparison sites:
www.moneysavingexpert.com/homeins

> 💰 Online shopping, including a list of shopbots
> for different things:
> www.moneysavingexpert.com/
> shoppingrobots

Super-savvy Shopping

Now let's step it up a bit and go somewhere
most people wouldn't dare. This is about
pushing the web to a higher degree using
cashback websites. These are essentially
advertising websites, but instead of keeping
the money they're paid by companies to
promote them, they give it to you. So if you
buy something or get a product from a
website having clicked from the cashback site,
it gets paid and you get some of it.

Therefore, once you've found the best
product for you (and always do that before
using a cashback site) then see if you can get
cashback on it. This isn't small change either:

it can be 4–5 per cent of the cost of what you're buying, or up to £100 per insurance product. So if you're getting new products or buying something online, step up the gain by getting a cut of the advertising revenue for yourself.

MoneySaving Web Resource

💷 Top cashback sites, including a list of comparison sites:
www.moneysavingexpert.com/cashbacksites

CHUTZPAH AND HOW TO HAGGLE

Chutzpah (pronounced *hoot'spa*), is a Yiddish word that basically means 'nerve'. If you're a person with chutzpah, it means you've got cheek – and this is a good

characteristic for MoneySaving. If you've
got the brass neck to demand them, you will
always get better deals. Having chutzpah
means having the confidence to ask for more
than you're being offered, or suggest you
should pay less for what you're getting.

Haggling is about getting what you want
by having the chutzpah to ask for it.

£ It's not about being rude or difficult.

£ It is about understanding that there's no
such thing as a fixed price, and that those
who don't ask don't get.

Haggling isn't always easy. Even if you try it
once a year on holiday, you're not likely to
feel 100 per cent comfortable doing it in
Woolworths.

The good news is that, increasingly, some
companies are used to hagglers, especially
those with call centres. A great place to try

your first haggle is with a mobile phone company or digital television or broadband provider; any deal where you have a contract which ends after about a year. This is because these providers are notoriously competitive, and always desperate to take customers away from one another.

The Haggling Challenge

When filming the Teen Cash Class programme, I challenged some of my students to try this. It didn't make the programme's final cut, but it was an incredibly useful lesson. What they didn't know was that the person they were talking to was an actor, specially briefed by me.

Martin:

Here's what I want you to do. This is the phone bill of a woman called Lesley Jackson. Call the company and get the

very best deal you can for her, by
haggling.

Robert:
So we talk to them and see if we can get
money off? Or extra stuff?

Martin:
You haggle for a better deal.

Robert (cheekily):
What if they won't give me one? Am I
allowed to tell them I might leave and
look somewhere else?

Martin:
I can't tell you that! This is a challenge!
That's for you to decide.

Sadly, in the challenge itself, Robert didn't
say he'd consider leaving – a pity, as it would
have got him top marks.

Remember, you're not locked into any company. They want to keep you, but they'll only fight for your custom if you make them. So if they don't give you the deal you want, ensure they know (politely) you'll consider leaving and then see what you get. Loyalty is for losers.

In fact, there's no such thing as the disconnections department. When you threaten to leave a provider, they often say, 'We'll put you through to customer disconnections.' Yet often the internal name for the department they connect you to is 'customer retentions'. This is because their job is to keep you as a customer and they have a LOT more power than standard customer services departments. If you're going to haggle, they're the best place to do it.

MoneySaving Web Resources

💷 Cashback sites:

www.moneysavingexpert.com/

cashbacksites

💷 Mobile phone haggling:

www.moneysavingexpert.com/mobilehaggle

💷 Car insurance:

www.moneysavingexpert.com/carins

💷 Online shopping:

www.moneysavingexpert.com/

shoppingrobots

💷 Digital television:

www.moneysavingexpert.com/digital

💷 Mobile phone cost cutting:

www.moneysavingexpert.com/mobphones

💷 Home phones:

www.moneysavingexpert.com/homephones

THE END... WELL, THE BEGINNING, REALLY

That's it. MoneySaving Lessons One to Three are complete. It's a tragedy that these are needed, but while our society has changed into a commercial, consumerist, corporate beast, our educational system hasn't caught up.

These lessons aren't taught in school. My main aim has been to teach you how to think about cash, your actions and our society in a way that protects your pocket.

I remember discussing with my publisher the title for this guide. They wanted it to be *The Three Most Important Money Lessons You've Never Been Taught* yet I didn't want the word 'money' added. After all, this is about far more than just 'money'; it's about how we live our lives.

And don't think that makes me overly materialistic; this is about empowerment. Whether you want to save the planet, have children, get help for mental health issues, give yourself a beauty makeover, decorate your house, get married or whatever – you need money. It's not the be-all and end-all, but it's the starting point for almost everything we do. It's time we accepted we need to work at our finances – both understanding that they need to be managed, and managing our understanding.

What Next?

The lessons don't end there. I've been a professional MoneySaver for seven years and an amateur for a lot longer, but I continually learn more and hone the techniques. The lessons I chose to share here were specifically to give you the raw ideas that'll see you through all aspects of finance. Yet every specific product has its own catches and you need to learn them carefully.

The Final Challenge: One that Pays You to Do It

Here's my final challenge. Look at everything you spend money on and see if you can get the same for less. You'll find the appendices of this book are designed to help you do just that.

There's no excuse. If you've found the time to read this, find the time to sort out your cash. So go forward, **beat** those companies at their own game and save yourselves oodles of dosh. Hopefully, you will pass this important message on to others too.

I hope you save some money.

Martin

HOW THEY DID IT

Before we go, just HOW did my 12 Teen Cash Class pupils make their £5,050 savings? Let's take a look at the areas where they made the biggest savings for their parents:

Number one was switching credit cards: my pupils saved a staggering £2,440 over a year by moving away from expensive plastic to better, cheaper alternatives. Well done!

In second place for curbing their parents' costs was changing insurance providers, whether car or pet: £830 over a year.

Next up was getting a cheaper deal for heating the home. By changing gas or electricity provider, some £450 was lopped off the bills.

Fourth was mobile phone savings: £120.

The remaining £1,210 was spread out across our other top tips.

GOOD DEBT OR BAD DEBT QUIZ (PAGE 49) ANSWERS

A. The holiday. Bad debt! The clue is in the question. If you can't afford it and don't need it, don't go into debt for it! A holiday is a luxury that you can live without for a few months while you save enough money to pay for it a better way.

B. A house. Good debt! Going into debt for some things is unavoidable, and a house is usually one of them. If you need to get a mortgage to buy your own place, find the best deal you can and consider it an investment in your future – though only do it if you can afford the repayments and you won't be hurting the rest of your finances.

C. A car. Good debt! If you need a car and can't buy one out of your own pocket, then borrow for one wisely. This isn't bad debt because having the car (as long as you get a good deal!) will improve your quality of life and enable you to earn money. Yet as you're borrowing, try and get the cheapest workable car, don't spend more than you need to, ensure you budget for your repayments, check that the interest rate is cheap, and pay it off as quickly as possible.

D. Party clothes. Bad debt! If you got this one wrong, shame on you! Feeling like you've got nothing to wear is no excuse for impulse shopping or buying something you can't afford. Even worse is putting this crazy purchase on a store card. Store cards have stupidly high interest rates. Remember, they're the devil's debt – designed to trap you!

APPENDIX ONE:

HOW TO GIVE YOURSELF A MONEY MAKEOVER

This is a full guide to giving yourself a money makeover. To make it easy to do, some of the content of the lessons has been repeated here.

The average person in the UK could give themselves an effective 25 per cent pay rise by stopping waste. This isn't by 'cutting out cappuccinos'; it's by systematically working through all bills and products to ensure you've got the best deal on everything. What follows is a five-step plan to overhaul your finances and save £1,000s.

Will It Really Make a Difference?

Be under no illusion: a full money makeover will take a good eight or ten hours, but it'll be worth it. In my TV series *Make Me Rich*, I was challenged to go to families' homes and save them as much as I could in a day.

The average saving was a little over £5,000 a year; and this was before I started to say 'cut back'.

Now, suppose by doing it yourself, you only do half as well, saving £2,500 (though hopefully you'll do better); compare that to what you earn! And remember this saving is tax-free so unless you're paid £3,500 a day (just under £900,000 a year) it's likely to be the best paid day of your year!

What if I Don't Have the Time?

Then make the time. This is incredibly important. However, if you simply can't right now and just need a quick MoneySaving hit then shimmy straight along to Step 2: Pain-free savings, and you should still manage to gain serious cash (*see page 118*).

Can I Get Someone to Do This for Me?

'Aarrgh!' I'm asked this all the time, and hate this question; asking it means you've missed the whole point of MoneySaving. The process doesn't just save you cash; it empowers you to understand how companies will take your cash through your ignorance, apathy and inertia. Yet even if that wasn't the case, there aren't any MoneySaving advisers, the service doesn't exist, and even if it did, their cost would eat up much of the gain.

STEP 1: DO YOU SPEND MORE THAN YOU EARN?

This isn't a trite question. Unless you know the answer, we can't work out how militant the savings must be. Standard

MoneySaving is about cutting your bills without cutting back; it involves changing your finances, not your life. Yet if after that you're still spending beyond your means, there's a major problem and cutting back may be necessary too; meaning lifestyle as well as MoneySaving changes.

Of course, those spending less than they earn may only need to free up wasted cash so it stays in their pocket, not in that of big companies. This is why it's important to know where you stand.

How to Find Out

There are two ways:

The BIG Danger Signal
Are you in debt? If you are, and can't answer the question, 'What are your debts from?' – in other words you didn't 'buy a car or a conservatory' but simply used cards or loans

to fill the gap – then this sounds an ear-piercing alarm.

It means your debt comes from systematically spending more than you earn. If this is the case, no further investigation is needed; we know the answer and you need to skip straight to pain-free savings (*see overleaf*).

Accurately Assess Your Spending

If you're not sure where your finances stand, you need to add it up. Using the Budget Planner on page 154 will help you to calculate your genuine annual income and how much more you spend than you earn.

This is the starting point of sorting out your cash, so spend the time to do the budget.

STEP 2: PAIN-FREE SAVINGS

The essence is simple: if you can get the same thing paying less, then do so. Yet it's not only about car insurance and credit cards. Saving money stretches to cutting childcare costs, finding cheaper contact lenses and checking your council tax bill. Below I've selected some ways that enable you to make big and easy savings on current outgoings.

Cut Your Household Bills

Gas and Electricity

You can cut your energy bills and get cashback on top in minutes. Remember, it's the same gas, same electricity, same pipes and safety; only the price and billing processes really change.

£ ww.moneysavingexpert.com/gaselec

£250 per year

Food Shopping
It's not about buying lower quality goods,
but beating the way supermarkets hypnotise
us into unnecessarily paying more.
ⓔ www.moneysavingexpert.com/
  supermarketshopping

£750 per year

Council Tax
The council tax system in England and
Scotland is fundamentally flawed. Many
people are in the wrong band. It only takes
ten minutes to check.
ⓔ www.moneysavingexpert.com/council

£300 per year
(and backdated reclaimed payout of £1,000s)

Home Phone and Broadband
There's no need to pay more than £20 per
month for a top home phone package and
broadband combined.
ⓔ www.moneysavingexpert.com/
  homephones

£200 per year

Childcare Costs

There's a little-known scheme called 'childcare vouchers' that enables you to pay for childcare from pre-tax income. While this doesn't sound much, the resultant savings are huge.

£ www.moneysavingexpert.com/childcare

£700 per year

Boiler Cover Costs

Don't assume you need to get boiler cover from the same company that supplies your gas and electricity.

£ www.moneysavingexpert.com/boiler

£100 per year

International Calls

You can call abroad for free via the internet, or call almost anywhere for 1p per minute via the normal phone.

£ www.moneysavingexpert.com/
  internationalcalls

£100s a year for regular callers

Should You Use a Water Meter?

If you have the same number or more of bedrooms in your house than you have people, you're probably better off with a water meter.

£ www.moneysavingexpert.com/water

Up to £200 per year

Digital Television

A simple phone call and the right haggling technique could halve your bill.

£ www.moneysavingexpert.com/digital

Up to £150 per year

Cut the Cost of Your Debts

Existing Credit Card Debts

Simply shift the debt to a new card at the cheapest possible rate.

£ www.moneysavingexpert.com/bts

£150 per £1,000 of debt

Mortgages

Mortgage savings can be massive, and they're much easier to achieve than you might think.

£ www.moneysavingexpert.com/
   remortgageguide

> *£1,000 per 1 per cent rate decreased per £100,000 owed*

Existing Loans

Cutting the cost of existing loans is much more difficult than mortgages or credit cards, but it's still possible.

£ www.moneysavingexpert.com/cutloan

> *If it's possible, £500 to £1,000 over the life of the loan*

Loan Insurance

Check if you've got insurance on any loans. If so, it's very likely you're being ripped off, and big savings are easy.

£ www.moneysavingexpert.com/
   loaninsurance

and see also www.moneysavingexpert.com/
reclaimppi

*Typically £1,000 to £2,000
over the life of the loan*

Stop Paying Minimum Repayments

Credit card minimum repayments are a
trap to keep you permanently in debt. It's
possible to escape this trap even if you can't
afford to pay more.

💷 www.moneysavingexpert.com/
minrepayments

*Up to £4,000 by the time
the debt is totally cleared*

Pay off Your Debts with Savings

Almost everyone with both debts and
savings is wasting a fortune. Pay off the
debts and save.

💷 www.moneysavingexpert.com/payoffdebts

Up to £100 a year per £1,000 of debt

Cut Your Personal Bills

Gym Costs

It's possible to get less than half price gym membership at Virgin Active, Cannons and LA Fitness with a special loophole.

£ www.moneysavingexpert.com/gyms

£200 per year

Mobile Phone

There's a white heat of competition in the mobile marketplace. Push the right buttons to stamp down the cost.

£ www.moneysavingexpert.com/mobphones
   and see also www.moneysavingexpert.com/
   freetexts

Up to £400 per year

Best Bank Accounts

You can get interest of 6 per cent or more or a 0 per cent overdraft without paying a fee.

£ www.moneysavingexpert.com/banks

£200 per year

Cheaper Prescriptions and Medications

If you regularly get prescriptions, use an annual certificate. Plus don't buy branded medicine: exactly the same things are available at a fraction of the cost.

£ www.moneysavingexpert.com/
prescription

£50 per year

Up Your Savings Interest

Never assume all banks are the same. The difference in the interest paid out is huge.

£ www.moneysavingexpert.com/saving and
see also www.moneysavingexpert.com/isas

£30 per year per £1,000 saved

Cheaper Contact Lenses

You can get exactly the same lenses for a huge discount by buying away from the high street.

£ www.moneysavingexpert.com/
health/Cheap-Contact-Lenses

Roughly £100 per year

Cheaper Petrol

Find the cheapest petrol station near you in seconds.

ⓔ www.moneysavingexpert.com/fuel

Savings of £100 plus per journey are possible

Cheapest Train Fares

The train ticket system is complex but play it right and there are massive loopholes to exploit.

ⓔ www.moneysavingexpert.com/trains

Savings of £100 plus per journey are possible

Are You Missing Out on Extra Money?

Can You Boost Your Income?

There are lots of ways to add to your income, whether it's home-working, using the web to profit or getting paid for your opinion.

ⓔ www.moneysavingexpert.com/makemoney

Up to £5,000 depending on your time and talents

Five-minute Benefit Check-up

Anyone with a family income of under £66,000 may be entitled to get benefits. Ensure you're not missing out.

£ www.moneysavingexpert.com/benefits

If appropriate you could be talking £1,000s

Get Paid to Spend

Stop using debit cards, cash and cheques for spending and use a cashback credit card – you get paid each time you spend. Very profitable as long as you always pay the card off in full.

£ www.moneysavingexpert.com/
cashbackcards

£150 extra cash per year

Stoozing

If you're financially savvy and debt-free it's possible to take a credit card's 0 per cent debts, save them at a high interest rate and make real money.

£ www.moneysavingexpert.com/stooze

£300 per year profit

Grant Grabbing

There are £1,000s of unclaimed grants out there for energy efficiency, homes, businesses and study.

€ www.moneysavingexpert.com/grants

Typical grants of £100 to £500

Recycle Old Mobiles for Cash

There are over 90 million old mobiles sitting in people's drawers; it takes five minutes to convert these to cash.

€ www.moneysavingexpert.com/ mobilerecycling

£10 to £100

Endowments. Did/Do You Have One?

If your endowment is underperforming and you weren't told this was a possibility, it was missold. Send a simple letter and you may be entitled to huge money.

€ www.moneysavingexpert.com/ missoldendowments

£3,000 to £15,000 back

Have You Moved Your Mortgage Company in the Last Six Years?

If so then you were almost certainly overcharged on the 'exit fee'; you should be able to get this cash back with a phone call.

£ www.moneysavingexpert.com/
mortgagefees

£50 to £150 for a phone call

Bank Charges. Have You Had Them in the Last Six Years?

If so then you may be able to reclaim them. This one will probably take a few hours to go through in its own right, but it's well worth doing.

£ www.moneysavingexpert.com/
bankcharges

Up to £10,000 depending on your charges

Have You Paid Credit Card Fees in the Last Six Years?

If you've paid charges for late payment or overspending; you can get up to six years' worth back.

£ www.moneysavingexpert.com/ccreclaim

Up to £5,000 depending on your charges

Cut Your Insurance Costs

Car Insurance

It's possible to easily cut car insurance costs. Don't think 'it's not time to renew now'; you can still ditch, switch and save.

£ www.moneysavingexpert.com/carins

Up to 50 per cent cheaper than existing policies

Home Insurance

Like car insurance you can ditch, switch and save at any time. Using the full system you

can sometimes get home insurance for under
£50 in total.

€ www.moneysavingexpert.com/homeins

*Up to 50 per cent cheaper
than existing policies*

Breakdown Cover

Forget the big boys. Similar cover, with full
service and just as quick of call-out times, is
available for a quarter of the cost.

€ www.moneysavingexpert.com/breakdown

£100 a year on full service policies

Life Insurance (level term)

Many people rightly get life insurance to
protect their loved ones. Sadly, banks take
advantage and often charge twice as much as
needed. Ditch, switch and save.

€ www.moneysavingexpert.com/levelterm

Over £5,000 during the life of the policy

Mortgage Insurance

Did you get your mortgage payment insurance from your lender? If so you're probably paying way over the odds, but it's easy to save.

£ www.moneysavingexpert.com/mppi

£300 per year

Mortgage Life Insurance

If your life insurance to protect your home is supplied by your mortgage lender, you're paying massively over the odds!

£ www.moneysavingexpert.com/lifeinsurance

Over £3,000 during the life of the policy

STEP 3: DO YOU STILL SPEND MORE THAN YOU EARN?

Now you've done all the main pain-free savings, your new expected monthly outgoings should be significantly lower. What to do next depends on you.

Were You Already Spending Within Your Means?

If so, you should now have more money to spend, save or repay debts. However, remember things change; you need to keep on top of your finances. Today's best deal isn't necessarily tomorrow's.

Yet even though you're now spending within your means; you may still be in debt or wanting to save quickly for something specific. In that case, some of the techniques in Step 4: Painful Savings may still be useful (page 136).

Were You Spending More than You Earned Before?

We now need to know if you've brought your spending under control. This again means calculating an accurate answer based on your new expenditure levels. If you did the Budget Planner earlier, all you need do is rework the values for areas where you've made savings. If not, then it's time to start the Budget Planner process (see page 143).

You may consider this to be a bit unnecessary. After all, you've done the savings, so do you really need an accurate answer? My response is an unrelenting yes. The reason is what's called a 'debt spiral', one of the nastiest, most unrelenting, life-destroying financial problems you can have.

You may feel this is over-dramatising. Yet when there's no money left, you can't borrow more, and the creditors are asking for money back that you've no ability to repay, it touches every element of your life.

Don't Get Into a Debt Spiral

You spend more than you earn

 You borrow to fill the gap

More of your income goes towards repaying debts

 You keep borrowing more to maintain your lifestyle

THE END RESULT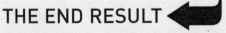

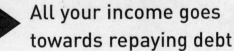 All your income goes towards repaying debt

 YOU'VE NOTHING LEFT

All this means we need to know whether you still spend more than you earn, so you need to fill in the Budget Planner on page 154. If it says you're now spending within your means... hoorah! You may still be in debt or wanting to save for something specific, so you may find some of the 'painful savings' below useful.

Alternatively, you may consider the job done. Yet even in that case, remember things change, and you need to keep on top of your finances. As I said before, today's best deal isn't necessarily tomorrow's.

If you're still spending more than you earn, there is no option – you need to rein in your expenditure, so keep reading...

STEP 4: PAINFUL SAVINGS

These are changes that involve curtailing or changing elements of your lifestyle. It sounds horrid, but actually it can be much easier than you think. Small changes on things you do regularly, such as cutting down from two takeaways a week to one, can save you £250 a year.

The place to start is www.moneysaving expert.com/stopspending, which is specifically designed to challenge your spending impulses, and includes The Demotivator, a tool to stop you spending what you can't afford. Yet cutting back your spending is all about asking yourself the right questions:

- Do you really need all your Sky TV channels?
- Can you make meals rather than get takeaways?
- Do you really need that cappuccino?
- Why not start making sandwiches for lunch?
- Do you need your weekly celeb gossip magazine?

(£) Do you need a car – could you sell yours?

(£) Could you get a second job?

(£) And why not stop smoking?

This boils down to asking two questions for every element of your life:

(£) Do I need it?

(£) Even if I do need it, can I still satisfy the need – even though it mightn't be as good – in a cheaper way?

What if All These Cutbacks Still Aren't Enough?

My first answer is 'try a little harder'. Many people think they've cut back on everything, but there are still little things that could go. Over time the little things add up.

If things are so serious, it's very likely you're also in significant debt. If that's the case and you can't afford to make even the minimum repayments on your standard outgoings, you need to take urgent action. There is a range of non-profit debt counselling agencies that will help you. For more on this go to www.moneysaving expert.com/debtproblems

Piggybank Budgeting

Budgeting isn't just a way of calculating your expenditure; it's also a way of controlling it. One of the ways to do this is to start living with the philosophy 'What can I afford to do?' rather than 'How can I do what I want for less?'

Now you know how much money you want to spend on different items, the aim is to make always knowing how much cash you have simple for you. To do this, set up a number of different bank accounts, each with money in it for a different purpose, so the money's effectively in little pots. When you get paid or earn the cash, have direct debits or standing orders shift the cash over to them from your main bank account within a day or so.

This is a bit like using a piggybank, putting money in different ones for different spending. Which accounts you choose depends on your personal priorities and spending habits. Choose whatever suits your lifestyle and makes it easier for you.

A simple example of six accounts:

- **£** **Bills (including mortgage)**
- **£** **Family food**
- **£** **Big purchases (sofa, car, kitchen)**
- **£** **Holidays**
- **£** **Christmas**
- **£** **Savings and emergency fund**

This means whatever is left in your main bank account is actually spendable each month. And you really know how much

money you have to spend at Christmas or
to go on your holiday – there's no fooling
yourself any more.

It's perfectly possible the end result of this
is that you can't afford the holiday you
wanted. More importantly, though, it means
that if you follow it properly you won't spend
what you can't afford.

APPENDIX TWO:

HOW TO BUDGET

This is a full guide to budgeting. To make it easy to do, some of the content of the lessons and money makeover have been repeated here.

$\mathcal{D}$rawing up a budget properly will answer two important questions for you:

(£) **Do I spend more than I earn?** This can lead to major problems, as continued overspending leads to serious debt. The Budget Planner will definitively answer this question and give you a realistic assessment of your finances.

(£) **What can I afford to spend?** The most important thing is to prioritise your expenditure and stick within your means. If you discover you're overspending, by correctly budgeting using the piggybank technique (*see page 139*) it should be easy to do this.

What's Different about this Budgeting Technique?

Traditional budgets fail as they concentrate on one month's expenditure, yet we don't always spend by the month. It may be weekly or, in the case of Christmas or summer holidays, annually. This leaves most budgets missing out a chunk of expenditure – and thus not adding up.

The Budget Planner is therefore designed so you can enter how often you buy certain items and, rather than the typical 20 categories of spending, has over 90 categories to ensure you don't miss anything.

Doing the Budget Planner accurately will take over an hour. It's best if you gather together your bank and credit card statements first, preferably the last three months' worth. Between them, they should list all standing orders and direct debits, and give you an accurate idea of what you spend.

For example, for food shopping, gather together all your receipts for the last three months, add up all food spending listed, then divide by three to reach your average monthly spend.

If you can, also gather together your payslips to establish exactly what you earn, plus any bills or other documents if possible (though your statements should also detail this information).

Get All the Calculations Done for You

While you can do it here in the book, even easier is to use the all-singing, all-dancing Budget Planner that will do it all for you. You can find it at: www.moneysavingexpert.com/budgeting

Tips for Filling Out the Budget Planner

£ **Are you doing it just for you or for your family?** It's very important to be consistent when budgeting. First decide who you're filling it out for: is it just for you or is it for your partner/family too? Finances often can't be separated, in which case you should sit down and do it together.

£ **MoneySave while you do this.** It's always surprising to see quite how many different things you spend cash on. Worse still is how much money you truly spend on them. Yet there are always ways to save. It's worth considering that as you write them down – are you getting the best value for your money? Can you get them cheaper elsewhere?

£ **Ensure items go in the correct column.**
Choose whether you most commonly
spend on something by the week, month
or year and fill that in – but do ensure you
have the right column.

£ **You can't put an amount in more than
one column.** So if, for example, you
always do a big monthly food shop and
then weekly ones too, you need to
calculate what you spend over a month
yourself using a calculator.

£ **Overestimate, don't underestimate.**
It's tempting to try and fool yourself by
underestimating your expenditure. This
is a MoneySaving sin, and you will be
punished. Try and be accurate and, if
you're not sure, guess larger not smaller –
that way you'll have cash left over and not
be short.

£ **Watch out for double-counting.** Some types of spending overlap into different groups; be careful not to count expenditure twice. For example, if you've included your car insurance in the motoring section, don't include it again under insurance.

£ **Pay special attention to credit card repayments.** The credit card section is designed for you to enter the cost of repaying your existing credit card debts. Don't confuse this with the type of spending where you simply use your credit card and pay it off in full. The best way to explain this is with an example. Say you spend £500 each month on food shopping that you pay for on your credit card but then pay off in full. This spending belongs in the food shopping column and not in the credit card column as, otherwise, you'll be counting it twice.

£ **Don't include company pension contributions in expenditure.** Pension payments are included in the expenditure section; if you send a cheque or have a payment from your bank account each month to pay into your pension, include it there. However, if your pension comes straight from your salary as a payroll payment, don't include it as, when you fill in the income section, you should just fill in the amount you receive after all deductions.

£ **Treat holidays carefully.** Remember that when you go on holiday, you'll have expenditure while you're away; but you also don't spend on the things you normally would. So you may want to reduce the amount you put in your holiday category by a little. For example, say you normally spend £100 per week on food shopping and £30 on petrol.

If you're abroad for the week, you won't spend this but you'll still be adding them in. Therefore, if the holiday cost £700 and you spend £300 you may be tempted to put £1,000 in – but actually you're saving £130 of normal expenditure so it should only be £870.

£ **Use the 'Odds and Sods' sections.** There are lots of categories in the Budget Planner, but it's impossible to include everything. At the end of each section there's an 'Odds and Sods' category. Take a minute to think if there's anything you spend money on that is missing – and include it there.

£ **Thoroughly double-check when you finish.** One small error, such as putting £1,000 annual holiday spend in the monthly column, can make an enormous difference. Before you finish the Budget

Planner, double-check everything is correct and you haven't missed anything.

Okay – now fill in just Part A of the chart. Once this is completed, work out what your real monthly spending is by filling in Part B, the 'monthly total' column. To do this you will (probably) need a calculator (remember, at www.moneysavingexpert.com/ budgeting there's an automated version you can use):

£ **For things in the 'per week' column:** Multiply the amount by 4.33 (the average number of weeks in a month) and put the answer in the 'monthly total' column.

£ **For things in the 'per month' column:** Move the answer straight over to the 'monthly total' column.

£ **For things in the 'per year' column:** Divide the amount by 12 and put the answer in the 'monthly total' column.

Budget Planner

	FILL IN FOR PART A			PART B	PART C
	Per week	Per month	Per year	Monthly total	Monthly desired
HOME					
Mortgage/rent					
Building and contents insurance					
Bank account fees					
Overdraft costs					
Council tax					
Water rates/meter					
Gas					
Electricity					
Oil					
Household maintenance					
Garden maintenance					
Cleaning					
Cleaning products					
Home phone					
Internet					
Mobile phone					
Other home					
TOTAL HOME					
INSURANCE					
Level term					
Mortgage payment protection					
Mortgage term					
Pet					
Travel					
Gas and plumbing/ boiler cover					
Other insurance					
TOTAL INSURANCE					

Budget Planner

	FILL IN FOR PART A			PART B	PART C
	Per week	Per month	Per year	Monthly total	Monthly desired
EATS, DRINKS AND SMOKES					
Food and household shopping					
Eating out					
Coffees/sandwiches/ snacks					
Drinks for home					
Drinking out					
Smokes					
Meals at work					
Other eats, drinks and smokes					
TOTAL EATS, DRINKS AND SMOKES					
TRANSPORT AND TRAVEL					
Breakdown cover/ roadside recovery					
Rail/bus/coach/ taxi travel					
Car maintenance					
Car insurance					
Car tax					
Parking					
Petrol/diesel					
Other transport and travel					
TOTAL TRANSPORT AND TRAVEL					

Budget Planner

	FILL IN FOR PART A			PART B	PART C
	Per week	Per month	Per year	Monthly total	Monthly desired
DEBT REPAYMENTS *(just the average amount repaid, not the total debt)*					
Car loan repayments					
Personal loan repayments					
HP repayments					
Credit card repayments					
Other loan repayments					
TOTAL DEBT REPAYMENTS					
SAVINGS AND INVESTMENTS *(how much you pay in, not how much is in there)*					
Regular savings					
Lump sum savings					
Mini cash ISAs					
Investments					
Buying shares					
Pension payments					
Other savings/investments					
TOTAL SAVINGS AND INVESTMENTS					
FAMILY					
Childcare/play schemes					
Babysitting					
Children's travel					
Laundry/dry-cleaning					
Nappies/baby extras					
Pocket money					
School meals					
School trips					
Pet food					
Other family					
TOTAL FAMILY					

Budget Planner

	FILL IN FOR PART A			PART B	PART C
	Per week	Per month	Per year	Monthly total	Monthly desired
FUN AND PROLICS					
DVD/video rental					
IT/Computing (e.g. anti-virus software)					
Hobbies					
Pet costs					
Shopping for fun					
Big days out					
Books/music/films/ computer games					
Cinema/theatre trips					
Family days out					
Satellite/digital television					
Subscription					
Television licence					
Other fun and frolics					
TOTAL FUN AND FROLICS					
HEALTH AND BEAUTY					
Fitness/sports/gym					
Private medical insurance					
Dental insurance					
Healthcare cash plans					
Beauty treatments					
Dentistry					
Haircuts					
Optical bills					
Complementary therapies					
Other health and beauty					
TOTAL HEALTH AND BEAUTY					

Budget Planner

	FILL IN FOR PART A			PART B	PART C
	Per week	Per month	Per year	Monthly total	Monthly desired
CLOTHES					
New clothes					
New children's clothes					
Work clothes					
Other clothes					
TOTAL CLOTHES					
EDUCATION AND COURSES					
Your courses					
School fees					
University tuition fees					
Other education and courses					
TOTAL EDUCATION AND COURSES					
BIG ONE-OFFS					
Christmas					
Summer holiday					
Winter holiday					
Birthdays					
Sofa/kitchen/television					
Wedding expenses					
Funeral expenses					
Other big one-offs					
TOTAL BIG ONE-OFFS					
ODDS AND SODS *(anything that doesn't fit elsewhere)*					
Regular charity donations					
Tax and NI provisions (self-employed only)					
Newspapers and magazines					
Other odds and sods					
TOTAL ODDS AND SODS					

Now total up each section and write the answer below:

Home total per month: _____

Insurance total per month: _____

Eats, drinks and smokes total per month: _____

Transport and travel total per month: _____

Debt repayments total per month: _____

Savings and investments total per month: _____

Family total per month: _____

Fun and frolics total per month: _____

Health and beauty total per month: _____

Clothes total per month: _____

Education and courses total per month: _____

Big one-offs total per month: _____

Odds and sods total per month: _____

Total Monthly Expenditure: _____

APPENDIX THREE:

GLOSSARY

Bad debt: When you borrow money for something you don't need or isn't worth it. When you use borrowing to fund a lifestyle that you can't afford.

Chutzpah: Nerve, bare-faced cheek. The guts to ask for a better deal.

Commercial debt: When you owe money to a company (e.g. a bank) and are charged a hefty rate of interest for it.

Companies: The opposition. NOT YOUR FRIENDS! Banks, shops and businesses of any kind... They are all out to get their mitts on your money.

Compound interest: The reason why a debt will cost you more if you take longer to pay it off. It's because you end up paying interest on the interest.

Credit card: A borrowing card. When you pay for something on a credit card, you go into debt for whatever you've purchased.

Debit card: A card that takes money directly out of your bank account. Allows you to pay for things in shops without using cash.

Debt: When you owe somebody cash.

Debt crisis: When you don't have enough money to repay your debts and other outgoings. If you hit debt crisis, you could lose everything.

Debt spiral: When you borrow money to finance a lifestyle you can't afford, and keep

having to borrow more to keep this going.
If you don't stop the spiral, it will lead to a
debt crisis (*see separate entry*).

Good debt: When you borrow money for a
good reason, in the right way (affordable and
as cheap as possible), having thought it
through carefully.

Haggling: Using chutzpah (*see separate
entry*) and your natural charm to talk
someone into giving you a better deal.

Impulse shopping: Very, very silly! It's
buying something without using my money
mantras to think properly first. Don't do it!

Interest: The cost of borrowing money. It's
usually given in the form of a percentage (the
interest rate). This is the percentage of the
original amount you borrowed that you will
have to pay back on top of your loan.

Losers: People who stay loyal to the same companies and think all offers are the same, and therefore never get the best deals.

Minimum repayment: The smallest amount per month that a credit card company will allow you to pay. Also, the cleverest invention EVER. Fall for this trick, and you'll be in debt for your whole life – because as your debt falls, so does the amount you're paying off.

Mortgage: A special loan that you get for buying a house. It's usually at a low rate of interest because if you don't pay up in the way the bank asks, they can take your house away.

Opportunity cost: When you have one thing but, as a result, miss out on having another. You can assess opportunity cost by asking yourself, 'Is it worth it?'

Overdraft: An amount of money that you can take out of your bank account even when there's no money in there. You need to agree this in advance with your bank, and they can charge you interest because they are lending you the money. It's a type of debt.

Screenscraper: A special type of website that will search the internet for a range of prices; literally scraping them off the screen of other sites.

Shopbot: A 'shopping robot' website that will search the web for the cheapest price on a wide variety of products.

Store card: A credit card you can only use in certain places. They have high rates of interest and are the devil's debt. Stay away!

Student loan: The low-interest loan that the government will give you to pay for going to university.

ACKNOWLEDGEMENTS

Thanks to ITV1's *Tonight* for commissioning the programme and the wonderful staff and pupils at St Simon Stock School in Maidstone where the Teen Cash Class took place, proving it is a worthwhile concept. Plus thanks to Laura Starkey and Sam Dunn for helping me turn the transcripts into this guide and my MoneySavingExpert.com team for all their constant hard work and dedication.

INDEX

(Page numbers in *italic* are glossary entries.)

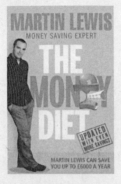

ABOUT THE AUTHOR

Ultra-specialised journalist, broadcaster and
financial campaigner, MoneySavingExpert
Martin Lewis, has his own Five TV programme
It Pays to Watch, regularly presents ITV1's
Tonight and is the regular expert on GMTV's
LK Today, Radio 2's Vine and Radio 1's
Whiley. His free-to-use, ad-free website
www.MoneySavingExpert.com is the UK's
biggest money website with over three million
visitors a month, and his weekly e-mail
newsletter goes to 1.5 million people.